The Boy and The Tree

poems by Ovsei Driz

illustrated by Victor Pivovarov

translated by Joachim Neugroschel

Prentice-Hall, Inc., Englewood Cliffs, New Jersey

THE BOY AND THE TREE

Poems by Ovsei Driz

translated by Joachim Neugroschel
illustrated by Victor Pivovarov

Copyright © 1976 Izdatyelstvo "Dye Tskaya Literatura."
Translation copyright © 1978 by Joachim Neugroschel

First American edition published 1978 by Prentice-Hall, Inc.

Printed in the United States of America   ·J

Prentice-Hall International, Inc., London
Prentice-Hall of Australia, Pty. Ltd., North Sydney
Prentice-Hall of Canada, Ltd., Toronto
Prentice-Hall of India Private Ltd., New Delhi
Prentice-Hall of Japan, Inc., Tokyo
Prentice-Hall of Southeast Asia Pte. Ltd., Singapore

10   9   8   7   6   5   4   3   2   1

Library of Congress Cataloging in Publication Data

Driz, Ovsei Ovseevich, 1908-1971.
   The boy and the tree.

   Translation of Mal'chik i derevo, a collection of children's poems
originally written in Yiddish.
   SUMMARY: A collection of children's poems written by a
Yiddish poet in the Soviet Union.
   [1. Yiddish poetry.   2. Russian poetry]   I. Title.
II. Neugroschel, Joachim.
PZ8.3.D835Bo   1978   839´.09´13   78-4119
   ISBN 0-13-080929-2

Table of Contents

TRANSLATOR'S NOTE:

Ovsei Driz wrote these poems in Yiddish, and they were published in a Russian adaptation in the Soviet Union.

My American adaptation is based on part of the Yiddish manuscript and the Russian version, and on the illustrations, which, of course, were done for the Russian text.

Thus, the final American version is really a synthesis of all three sources.

J.N.

The Boy and The Tree

Tree, tree,
Give me a plum.
Silly boy, don't be dumb,
I'm an apple tree.

Let me live
A little bit longer,
And I'll give
You
An apple or two
For your hunger.

Writing

The bricklayer writes
A line that won't fall.
His lines build up high
Into a brick wall.

The shoemaker writes
Nails into hide.
His lines are straight,
Just like a road.

The dressmaker sews
On her sewing machine.
A polka dot dress
Can now be seen.

The blacksmith with a hammer
Bangs out lines.
And the grasshopper hops
And the moonlight shines.

Garbage

Big and little children
Run about.
They gather garbage
That people throw out.
A bike,
An iron,
A fork,
A door.
A teapot
That's not
In use anymore.

Children, tell us,
What happens
To garbage?
It's crushed,
And mushed.
It's bashed
And smashed.
And what do they do?
They make something new.
A bike that bikes.
An iron that irons.
A fork that forks
And a door that opens
Quietly.
A teapot that makes
Nice hot tea.

Not So Easy

I bought a brass trumpet
And I blew it as hard could be.
But I couldn't play the trumpet.
It's not so easy, you see.

I had a pair of slippers,
The leather as good as could be.
But I couldn't dance in the slippers.
It's not so easy, you see.

I had a needle and thread,
And a thimble too, for me.
But I couldn't sew with the needle and thread.
It's not so easy, you see.

The Gramophone*

Laugh if you like,
Or cry or hiss.
Listen to that
And listen to this.

I open up
And I turn on
Our old, old
Gramophone.

First it grinds
And first it seems
As if it's full
Of lima beans.

Like a hailstorm
On the slats,
Listen to this
And listen to that.

Then all at once
Its iron voice
Begins to sound
And to rejoice.

Like a bumblebee,
Like a wasp, like a drone,
It hums and hums—
Our gramophone.

It rocks and wobbles,
It limps and hobbles.
It grinds along.
Just hear its song.

I bang on it,
The lazybones.
It looks so crazy—
Our gramophone.

Laugh if you like,
Or cry or hiss.
Listen to that
And listen to this.

*old-fashioned wind-up phonograph

I Think About The Things I Want

I've done my work.
It's time
To climb
Into bed.

But here I lie
And think
About what I
Would like.

If I like,
I think about bears,
And stars,
And squirrels and foxes
And a pair
Of boxes.
And about
What appears
Once in a thousand
Years.

I think about
A cat on a cloud,
A goat,
Oh my,
And a dragonfly,
And I float,
And everything floats.
And the stars dance
And the bears prance.
And so do the foxes
And the boxes
And the dragonflies
In the moon.
And soon
I close
My eyes.

The Forest Clock

Just think, just hear, just dream with me.
I stand on a chair and guess what I see.

I take a magic leap and I land
In the heart of a forest, and there I stand.

The eternal trees, they sway and rock,
And near a brook, I see—a clock!

It's made of pine, with a shingle roof,
And a mill wheel moves the hands of wood.

Now a key is grating in the silent hut,
And a shutter opens up like a nut.

And then a cuckoo slips right out,
It calls: Cu-koo! Cu-koo! And turns about.

Now try to think, and guess if it's true—
The thing that I would like to do.

I'd like to stand upon a rock
And pile a clock upon the clock.

And then another clock on top,
And then another—I'd never stop.

More and more, and higher and higher,
Clock on clock, and I'd never tire.

Another and another one,
Till my forest clock reaches the sun.

The Mischievous Flower

The flower was pink
And frail, and,
I think,
Like a child's hand.
Five petals shut
Into a fist so small.
But
At night, she wouldn't open
At all.
Despite my pleas
She would only tease
With all her beauty.
"Well,
Can you tell
What's in my fist?"
Then, in the morning mist,
At the first ray
Of the new day,
She slowly unclenched
Her fist and set free
Three
Tiny birds that zoomed
Into the sky. Then she
Bloomed
And forgot
All about
Me.

Little Goat

Little goat, nanny goat gray,
Saw a wagon filled with hay.

Oxen pulled it slow and steady,
But the nanny goat was ready.

The wheels turned round and round,
The goat gave chase without a sound.

Little goat, nanny goat gray,
Began to munch the crunchy hay.

Who Slept Where

In the huts of clay
The swallows lay.
The horse slept in the stable,
The bees in the dark hive,
The dog under the table.
The chickens had the best space,
Under the brood hen's wing.
What a warm place!

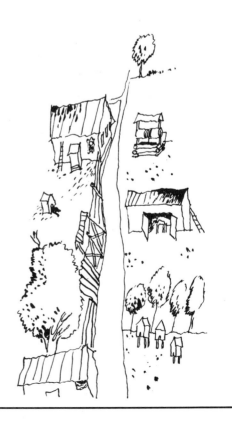

Watch The Birdie

Tom the grey cat said to his wife,
It's time we had our picture taken,
Together with the kittens,
And we'll have it for life.

The photographer was a goat.
He took off his coat.
He set the camera up high
And put in the film—oh my!

Then he scurried, quick and deft,
Gave everyone a chair.
Tom to the right, his wife to the left,
And the kittens in front, my dear!

The family was ready.
The goat said: "Look at the birdie!"
He took his time
So that everything would be fine.

But then it happened: It was awful,
It was downright unlawful.
The camera started to sway.
The birdie flew away.
And the picture will be taken
Another day.

Duba, Duba, Duba,* Ukrainian Folksong

Duba, duba, duba,
Over green grass,
Over green gardens,
The ravens pass.

Duba, duba, duba,
Someone wants to scare them,
He goes to the meadows,
And sticks in a stick.

Duba, duba, duba,
Cover me up,
With black scarves,
And all kinds of stuff.

Duba, duba, duba,
I stand up high,
A scarecrow all day,
And the ravens fly,
Till I scare them away.

*Refrain, like *tra la la*

At the Seashore

I was playing by the sea,
In warm and lovely weather,
And I picked up stones for me,
Black and white like seagull feathers.

But the things I like more
Are the shells on the shore.
They look like pockets, nice and small,
And I love them all.

I put one shell to my ear,
And I think I can hear
A star breathing there,
A living star. But where?

The fishes and the fishermen
Are laughing at me
Because I look for stars
In the depth of the sea.

Lullaby

Sleep my child, my little boy.
Fall asleep in your bed so white.
A tree will grow, just like a toy,
And a dream will fly through the night.

You'll have a crown of noodles,
And a ring of crusty dough,
The smell of a knish, the hole of a bagel,
A spicy wind and roasted snow.

Close your eyes, just go to sleep,
And no eyes will look at yours.
The night is long and dark and deep,
But you'll see the dream that soars.

Knish is Yiddish and Russian for a baked cake of dough
or mashed potato.
Bagel is Yiddish for a very heavy donut-shaped roll.

Temple Israel

Minneapolis, Minnesota

IN HONOR OF THE BAT MITZVAH OF
CARA LORRAINE GREENE
BY
KIM & CLIFF GREENE
JUNE 8, 1991